Drive By Heart

Drive By Heart

Poems by Michael Milburn

Word Press

Published by Word Press
P.O. Box 541106
Cincinnati, OH 45254-1106

ISBN: 9781934999677
LCCN: 2009934894

Poetry Editor: Kevin Walzer
Business Editor: Lori Jareo

Visit us on the web at www.word-press.com

Acknowledgments

Thanks to the editors of the journals in which the
following poems appeared:

Burnside Review: "Custody"
Broken Bridge Review: "Slacker," "Teller"
Confrontation: "Freeze Frame"
Harvard Magazine: "At the Vietnam Memorial"
Harvard Review: "Accompaniment," "Loose Ends"
Madison Review: "At 80," "Not This Child"
Mississippi Review: "Passage"
New England Review: "In the Frame," "Poem in Place of
        Goodbye," "Words for a Child"
Onthebus: "Notice," "Preserved"
Ploughshares: "Toothbrush Time," "Location, Location"

Some of these poems appeared in the chapbook, *The
Blessings of Motion and Silence* (Finishing Line Press,
Georgetown, KY).

To my sisters, Nancy and Tina

Contents

It's not only its own life that man's body has to endure.

Charles Simic

I

Passage

At a party a man I once liked remarked,
"I haven't seen you since you became
a father. No doubt you've faced it
with your own low-key, sensible reserve."
He said it to be mean, I thought,
but approached me smiling later to chat:
his wife had abandoned him to mingle.
At such comments one nods, ponders,
slowly drilling each word for its ore.
Low-key. Sensible. Reserve.
I remembered a cozy New Year's Eve
in their Cape Cod house, swapping
drug tales—college LSD trips, the exploits
of stoned friends. Me conspicuously silent.
Earlier, he'd proffered a thick joint.
When I refused, he said, "Well, I didn't
count on this." They smoked while
I sat with my drink, trying hard to keep up
with their hilarity. At midnight, everyone
embraced except me. The next day
we walked the beach, his wife and mine
up ahead. I spoke vaguely and he pressed
for precision—one of those fastidious minds—
until I, hopeless with facts, shut up entirely.
At the party the same thing—my comment,
his querying, querying. I tried to see myself
as low-key, sensible, reserved in a good sense,
facing fatherhood like that, as when I calm
my son's fiery panic at bedtime.
Then my traits serve as routes into
the world, no less than that man's blunt,
plaguing conversation, or a small boy's
pounding at the bedroom door.

In Common
for J.C.

We lay on the sunny grass full of complaint,
braiding our marriage tales
through the noon hour—the moody wife,
the constant child, a life social or solitary,

subtly flexing our marriages
against these blows as if to say,
I'm strong, I beat my chest.
And you did beat yours and it held;

for all I pressed you it held,
and now I see the iron there. Yet mine,
like a bridge slammed
too long by jolting trucks,

gave way invisibly inside, shocked
to powder and disintegrating outward,
until when the cracks showed
the heart was already gone.

Stress—I watched yours vibrate
into the midday sun, as you shook
your marriage free of it. Mine
piled up inside, though I talked on,

like some so-called expert
on what makes a structure succumb,
hotly predicting the damage
long after the damage is done.

Freeze Frame

Some comb the past for blame,
forever reviewing the tape
like Monday Night Football
to say, "There, stop it for a second,

the injury occurred there." Others
know deep down they'll be hurt,
say so and it happens.
In the kitchen today,

remembering a conversation
from six months ago, I stopped
the tape, but couldn't tell
from the angle if you were

pushing or I was simply falling
and would have crumpled anyway.
I'd like to have you over to see,
run the tape and you could cue me

to stop it and say what we're doing,
like football where someone watching
from a distance decides and it's over.
They just decide and it's over.

Adoptee

When I first saw you at the meeting,
diving from your mother's lap,
you gaped like a visitor
from another land,

the one she'd stepped off
the plane from that morning,
rushing to work to show you off.
You looked, to put it bluntly,

extremely Chinese, not just foreign
like our émigré receptionist,
but like you were still in China,
toddling by a roadside

while your new mom
strode through rice fields
to claim you. Just then
the idea of a world

where a child
could fall asleep in Hunan
and awaken in Hartford
seemed as preposterous

as the fact that today,
twelve years later,
you'd prance before me
in braids and cut-offs,

whiffing on a soccer ball
and shouting, "Shit." Now that's,
as someone murmured
when you entered, a miracle.

Chaperone

Four of us laugh at Scrabble
as a dance throbs next door:
Sally, Tim, Michelle and me,
their English teacher, host

of this designated quiet room.
Others stop in, sweating, happy,
and one girl, shy in class
but dressed tonight

in a tight blouse and skirt,
presses close to whisper
in my ear. Her hot breath shocks me.
The walls hold snapshots

from another teacher's life—
family, pets—and posters
meant to make math
seem silly and fun.

We play for hours under
the fluorescent lights:
Sally, the plump poet,
sophisticated; Michelle,

hampered by a nervous silliness,
a plague to boys; and Tim,
whose voice swoops and cracks this year
like radio static—each feels blessed

just to sit and play,
not gyrate under strobes.
When the wall clock clicks to ten
we fold the board and stand,

like four Bingo veterans. Outside,
kids call wisecracks as I unlock my car.
Hot Breath hugs me good-bye.
They all seem drunk on something—

music, the April evening,
or what I in my own giddiness
might call youth, though never
to their rolling eyes.

Poem in Place of Goodbye

Taking another sip you'd murmur
that you remembered everything, and I'd laugh
at your tipping, swaying speech.
Our lunches, punctuated by wine,
always ended with you swerving off to teach,
your stage-fright dulled by drinks. Then last month
when I phoned to say I was moving,
and ask you something damned important
about a job, you could barely speak. I asked anyway
through your haze of giddy confusion
and then hung up. We made a lunch date;
you never came, and called me to make another.
I waited as the restaurant filled. At half-past
you appeared, not weaving as I'd feared,
but slack, dead-eyed, and uncombed, your eyes'
black circles darker. You lagged a step, a whole
sentence, the waiter repeating the menu to you
like some aged, forlorn thing. I sat sullen,
sick of it, while you gazed at me,
half-grasping your disgrace
and half still in bed. You kept spooning soup,
pouring it over yourself,
and at the door handed the soiled tray
to the cashier who angrily flung it
in the obvious trash can. "I don't know
what I've been up to," you muttered,
walking to your car. Did your students
or colleagues dread you as much as I dreaded
your next visit or call? I wanted to say
that someone should care for you, a friend, but of course

I'm your friend, I should care, yet here
I'm two months moved with no goodbye,
still tempted to reach and retrieve you
as you waver from view, bawled at by a car horn,
on your way for good this time, on your own.

Loose Ends

Sealing the last cartons, he studied
his beloved bedroom view over roofs
and contiguous backyards, chimneys
piping smoke as he'd dressed winter mornings.

Below, she knelt gardening with a broken look.
The boy's shadow crossed
the playhouse window, then trailed him
up the dirt hill to hug her, crying,

in his wide arms. So their last day
gave way to its last night, blackening
yard after yard, picnic table, playhouse,
and summer balcony. When she stood in the door

to say goodnight, he made himself
barely look away from the TV.,
worked the house key from its tight ring,
and pressed the light.

Not This Child

Not this face drained of mischief,
these ivory arms or blond brow.
Not these limbs stretched in an x,
these scabbed knuckles

or fingernails clipped blunt
by school decree. Not this fist
crammed with pillow,
nor one rickety tooth.

Not this child but his world
scrapes me sore, makes me
swear and state what he
can't do, can't do, can't do.

His teacher with defeated sigh.
His classmate with clawed cheek;
her sputtering mother. I would
break them all back like branches

to blaze a life as welcoming
as this sleep, in which he lies,
buffeted, breathing in gusts,
like something tossed from the sea.

I would lash him fast
to my ledge of hip
and fend them off
with my free arm hacking.

So furious, so flushed
with love, I brush
his temple with my finger
and touch a spot more tender

than any of their hearts, beating
through my hands like blood.
Little hurricane, spend your winds
in my grateful waters.

Unmarried

I found myself laughing
as if I were there again
beside you laughing.

In the garden, videotaping
our wedding rehearsal,
your sister made us keep

repeating the kiss,
and watching it later
I kept rewinding

to find any hint
of your later loss of love,
but you kept on kissing and laughing.

I'd found the unmarked tape
and put it on, stepped
out of the room for a moment

and heard the brittle voices
and birdsong
and Dev's tentative sax, and knew.

I was surprised I could watch it,
not just with interest,
but with laughter

and a manageable sadness—
meaning, I guess, I'm over you,
I don't love you any more,

despite this evidence
from outside my heart
of how much I once did.

Custody

On TV it's where they drag bad men to,
hands locked behind in upside-down prayer:
you can't hurt anyone, or they you,
Attica and Oswald notwithstanding.

Kids share the term with villains,
led off feeling guilty or at risk.
Divorce-speak distinguishes Legal
and Physical. My son, for example,

isn't with me now, just his battered
orangutan and a huge inflated ball.
His presence, growth, belong
to Mom (Physical), but she can't

choose a school or make him Mormon
without my say (Legal). In the old
"Superman," when the Man of Steel
said "Those men are in custody,"

Miss Lane felt safe and wiped her brow.
So parents hope to feel, papers signed:
we can't hurt you now, nor you us,
Attica and Oswald notwithstanding.

Luminary

The last night of our summer together
I turned from his bed to discover him
climbed with a sly smile into mine.
The streetlamp that blinds me so I pile

pillows against it hit his face on one side,
his eyelids kindled by light. There,
with him lit like a jewel, I said goodbye.

These quiet cherishings, at visit's end,
before the teary airport or car window
embrace, when I imprint upon myself
his huge, altering presence, are like

goings off to war: a son visits his father;
a father says goodbye, as odd to me as
sane men killing: a corruption of God's world.

Then he returns and we wear each other
like old shirts—he bends to fit his TV. chair,
slides into bed where the streetlight burns him
into my eye, and I pile no shield against it.

Unaccompanied Minor

She scans the crowded tarmac,
passengers dragging suitcases,
leaning into wind. Sensing her panic,
I point out an attendant and two boys,
her son and mine, escorted
to a small propeller plane
now lowering its flimsy stair. I trace for her
the runway they'll taxi down
almost to the end, a single taillight
visible beyond the stacked jets,
before rocketing back toward us.

Saying goodbye in the parking lot,
I want to tell her how her day will drag
from here, how she'll try to work,
but go to bed and cry instead,
how housecleaning helps,
and exercise, anything purgative,
like the phone call at bedtime
to tell him that she misses him,
and sleep, though not the moments
before or after sleep, especially not these.

Notice

The annulment notice came today,
signed by the bishop, stating that
what we did on that day ten years ago
we did not do, undid, never happened.

Ten years! I'd forgotten the date,
but not even relearning it
could move me. Then they named
the place, not just the town but the inn,

which made me sadder, madder
than any of their questionnaires
inviting my rebuttal or response.
Why, I remembered the trees,

the tall green trees and blankets
of September light, a pond with lilies,
glassed porch, champagne, my quarreling siblings
and best friend, best man, now dead.

I remembered my suit and white car,
my nervous night before, a prayer
the minister read, the chubby minister
who everyone said looked like my brother.

That day began, if nothing else, my past
ten years, steering me toward this moment
like my mother waving her handkerchief
in the landscaped drive. I shoved

the letter in a box marked DIVORCE,
along with a sheaf of legal papers—deals,
decrees, the stuff of many tears—clicking it
closed for good, for real. This happened.

Off Season

It's his only exercise
and one he can't perform alone
so on weekends
we drive to the beach—
kids, grandkids, spouses
and Grandpa limping
into the sun. The boys
sprint down, sneakers
soaked immediately,
no pause even in January.
I walk, dragged by dogs,
beside my sister
while another sister
matches his pained shuffle behind.
He never makes the river
and we've long since turned back
to meet him when he turns back.
The dogs fight in bursts
and race around his legs,
so someone always
shadows his arm. He can't see
the dune break and must be
helped to navigate snow
leading to asphalt, but still
he falls, a boot breaks ice
and he kneels like a man shot;
his faint, focused sense of where he is
gets overwhelmed
and he can't buy a firm place
for his feet, sags
dependent on too-weak arms.
How could a man never
in the same atmosphere
as humiliation flounder so?

One helps him up,
pulls the dogs away,
two tow him out
of the snow and then go on; the dogs
lie wagoned among each other,
cars idle with doors wide and welcoming,
as voices talk loudly
to guide him from fence
to fender to safety inside.

911

By now the paramedics know her
and know she'll scorn their offer
of an ambulance, so, satisfied
with her competence, they leave.
It's hard enough waking
head against the toilet
and nightie hiked for a pee
without two flashlights
wagging in your eye. For all
his Wall St. gruffness
Dad can't boss her,
and when she says no hospital,
she just wants her own bed,

he goes mute, hands clasped
as she wanders the edge
of consciousness, his silence
the equal of her weeping
when he falls after a misstep
of the feet, not brain. Tomorrow
calls will circle again among
siblings who've woken
to a thump and found her
staring up from tiles, dazed
and shivering or out cold,
Dad in mournful vigil,
too meek to squeal,
both of them, for the first time,
working together.

Words for a Child

Slamming into my room
I shove hands against eyes
while he trembles downstairs,

chin dropped to chest, a cold
scowl aging his face. I check
my heart, blood, and breath,

wishing I knew a test
to pronounce myself human again
to speak to him, to name

what makes me fall so fast
toward rage when he won't
mind or listen. "Don't get

mad, don't get mad," he begs
after every accident. But look
at this man clenched on the bed,

fists binding fury to his head,
wishing it was enough to love
and apologize, sworn

to grit patience. Once again
my will and I have brawled into
the room and toppled to the bed

to fight hand to hand—"Don't get mad"—
and once again, god damn it,
I have won.

Slacker

Drifting into class late he slides into the seat
furthest from mine, shielded by loud girls
and with a sightline to his friend, studious,
but always willing to join him in a smirk
over a classmate's or my stupid comment.
He never sheds his pillowy parka or opens
his notebook except to check his next class,
whispers curt answers when called upon,
then smiles sleepily, gazing at the ceiling.
Colleagues swear that he gets high at home
mornings after his mother leaves for work,
that he's given up on school and they on him,
and I too no longer coax or scold, as bewildered
by this waste as by myself at his age and how little
I cared, how single-mindedly and with what
passion and ingenuity one can simply not care.

Len

He hangs out with the home-before-sports
effeminate nerds—not brainy
math or computer geeks, but poets,
pubescent Oscar Wildes. I pass them
on my way to coach: my spitting,
cursing jocks loathe Len's crowd. This fall
he rinsed his pale hair darker;
his silk shirts defy '90s grunge.
His gaze and tone have settled
into a winter of condescension,
outscorning even the cocky jocks
grunting their contempt.
When they speak in class
he flings me looks—impatient,
murderous—and proffers, unassigned,
poems called "A Weary Ramble
Thru My Fucked Up Life."
A new term brings lavender hair
and a nose ring. Len sighs, pointing,
when I walk in: "Lavender hair? Nose ring?
Comment." "Looks great," I say,
and in future weeks praise
new earrings, an overnight return
to blond, and Dracula-drip mascara:
looks great. And truly, make-up, jewels,
salon insouciance, become him,
but not those trenches of
dried muscle paving his biceps,
soft as my ten-year-old son's.
Len's rolled sleeve pleads *comment*
and I ask, "Is this suicide?"
"No, just some adolescent
mutilation thing." Len's thing,
it seems, is to keep shocking,

changing, flexing power
in those pasty arms, which once baked
Christmas treats for teachers,
topped by a crafts collage,
the jocks sneering
as Len, gloved in fudge,
forced popsicle sticks into
a snowman's temporary smile.

Visit

Slowing to the curb
I check his window light,
silhouetted photos
and shells lining a sill,
unkink the drive
from my spine, climb
and enter, climb
in socks with the dog
clicking behind. He's
a lump in the tumbled bed,
head cockeyed, mouth
flopped open in a snore.
Blankets bind his thighs.

I slip arms under
and slide him, hand
beneath his neck,
hand to his back,
swipe hair aside
to kiss his throat, like
bone china, as his eyes
lift to my sweatshirt,
his muscles to the tilt
of my cradling him; he hoops
his arms through mine,
legs cinched tight
as a girth, and whispers
"Daddy" as we sway
into the corridor.

At Eighty

A surgeon cracked his toes
with a mallet so he shuffles
in sliced sneakers, face
too veined to show the pain

that trails him like his sick, old,
starving retriever, Samson.
As he hoists the frying pan
near his chin and bends to read

the oven knob, grease spits
past his eyes. The pan shakes;
everything shakes—hands flap up
to grip mine, head shudders

into an anecdote at supper.
His spine's a rusted wire
that won't bend straight—toppling
after a late pee he flails

like a sodden turtle,
unable to flip or rise. Blood
drips behind his eyes,
there's blood in his eyes;

thus the newspaper clasped
to his face, head tipped
to dimming books like earth
leaning toward autumn. If I were God,

I'd piece him together
like a porcelain man,
knead his toes straight,
smooth his spine, still

with a touch his fluttering hand,
and sponge and seal
his eyes; I'd re-ignite
his roaring soul. Instead, I slide

a pen into his open palm,
a glass to catch his wine,
my hand in his shaking
hand, ready for goodbye.

Toothbrush Time

You claimed as the one worth
of your regrettable childhood
the knowledge you'd gained
to make another's childhood
exemplary. You found yourself
quite able to withhold

any emotion except love.
You were a rod, your son's rod,
your practiced calm his confidence,
solace, and security. From books
you learned carrot and stick,
the four-year-old's embracing

egotism, that rising above
on the parent's part which says
(as the toothbrush roams
the mouth, drawn out for chatter,
complaints, instant tears) it's
not him, it's his age.

But no books ever blessed
your rage. You might have flashed
with anger—then they said don't
punish yourself. Fury might inch
like mercury to your lips—
then they explain disabling

the bomb in two paragraphs.
But at bedtime, as you crumple
with sleep from his three
bad dreams the night before,
the day's dreaded last chore
arrives with a howl on the word

brush, and you grind bristles
over lips, bending his clenched
body. Then, nothing you have
ever felt or lived or read
will let you shout, *just brush
your goddamn teeth*,

least of all him, who curls
his lip down to pout,
"You don't love me 'cause
you yell at me," and sleeps,
leaving you awake, ashamed,
all evening in revenge.

Drive by Heart

I.

On Sunday trips home
after time with him,
memories tumble behind:
his gorgeous heaviness
in a hug, a headlocked,
leg-wrapping hug
when I creep in late
on a Friday; his roars
as he watches Stan vex Ollie
on TV. At bedtime,
his sorting of bodies—him, me,
and the fretful dog.
"Damn it, Grace lay
in my spot again,"
hurling his face
to the pillow. Thumb
his belly till a giggle
rips through the anger.

II.

Route 17 west into sunset,
through the Catskills,
along the Beaverkill,
halfway home by Roscoe.
Beside me on the front seat
the soft stamp of his head
where my finger earlier
swirled his hair, and Grace,
unbidden, circles out space
for his missing self.

II

Puzzle

Hoping to re-piece you into
someone I could remember,
I summoned a photo
from your living room—

studio posed with you
so dangerous in black. I retold myself
stories you'd told,
fumbling for your voice

as if to fasten it to words
and speak to myself as you.
But I made the wrong person,
slapping on flaws and failures

out of the rot of my old confusions. Finally,
flipping through old thoughts of you,
I uncovered one I'd forgotten,
the time I kissed you and lowered

my cheek to your face, my face
to your collar, as your head
fell against mine
and we both stopped talking.

I could feel, hear, taste,
and smell you then, everything
but see, and that's how
I best see you now, whenever I desire.

Preserved

When Nancy brings the video out,
years of brittle spools copied onto
one cassette, we all watch.
Dad sits too, blind, a book-on-tape
shouting through headphones,
pausing to grumble questions
when we laugh or exclaim.
"There's Grandpa," my son calls,
and there he is: hair slate black,
belly like a washboard. "That must be
Bermuda, 1950," Mom murmurs.
He's thirty-two, all movement,
slapping a polo ball,
clowning with a shotgun
as he picks off clay pigeons
flung into the sky. And here
he nestles a newborn
for the camera. "You look like me,"
my son says, nudging me.
When the screen switches abruptly
to snow, Mom sighs and I flick it off. The boy sniffles
and goes over to rest his head
on the swelled stomach. "Poor Grandpa,"
he whispers. The old man
touches his hair. "Hello, small grandson," he says, startled,
swinging his head toward the mute TV.
"Is it over?"

Incident

An eighth grader told her mother
that while her disabled teacher
wrote equations on the board
a boy lurched across the room,
fingers crooked like talons, miming
legs in braces and misshapen hands.

The principal called two meetings:
with faculty to organize response
and with students to discuss
the perils of intolerance. The phrase
"a learning experience" tumbled
approvingly from teachers' lips,
grudgingly from kids'. All week
I peered at the culprit, wondering
where his evil lurked: not in his
fair-minded observations
on English literature,
or his perceptive kindness
toward friends, or even
his alert and with-it parents,
schoolteachers themselves.

During the impromptu assembly,
he shrank against the gym wall,
no trace of cruelty in his downcast eyes,
and when a colleague muttered
that stupidity was more like it,
I agreed, wondering whose.

Being There

Stopping after work to fetch my son
from sports or school field trips,
I'd spot her helping teachers
or in the stands watching her son. A baby
slept in a harness around her neck.

I guessed her age as early twenties,
could as easily imagine her dangling
bare legs off a tailgate on prom night
as cheering an awkward son's tumble
after grounders. She looked weary,

as if the kids weighed her down
more than physically,
but back then I thought
of all full-time parents
as steeped in drudgery.

After my divorce and move away
I spent ten years driving back
on week-ends to visit my son. One day
her face came into focus in a restaurant.
In the decade she'd lost her youth,

utterly lost it; even before I spotted
the teenager, confident and muscular now
in a high school baseball jersey,
my first thought was
there's a woman with children.

When he stood to clear the dishes,
she smiled at him as at a man, not a child.
I thought of how well she must know him,
every inch of skin and insecurity,
as well as I wish I knew my son

through daily exposure.
Why hadn't I seen that this
was what she was cultivating
years ago? Why didn't I know about
the simple miracle of presence?

Half Empty

He's better at this than I am,
lives further away, but visits
more often and stays longer,
then flies home and reads
his daughter to sleep by phone.
When I compliment him,
he says "I've had practice,"
describes a previous divorce,
another child, grown now,
the same bi-coastal deal.

He's proud of this. The visits,
the phoned goodnights, all
make him feel (and others say)
he's a perfect absent father. To him,
it's something he does right,
does well, something fixed,
not broken. To me, it is
what it means to be broken.

Universal Butterfly

Beyond bay windows
a tiny Russian girl
grasps for butterflies
on the lawn. Her print dress

flares and stays flared
when she tumbles off
sturdy white legs.
Her new mother

calls curt scoldings
and an old golden
retriever comes over
to let his head be hung on

by a Russian child
fighting to rise.
Of the big and bounding
other dogs she shows

no fear, ambles
at the center
of their clamor
like a tamer.

Her brother gallops
through a sprinkler,
forgetting his mother's
charge to watch her;

he's from Milwaukee,
his mother's from Virginia,
and his father, my brother,
was bred, like me, among

butterflies and dogs
on this Long Island lawn.
From their tale of trains,
villages and guides

I haven't placed
what Russian town she's from,
but love how
they guided her through

newly opened galleries
as she leads her father now
through familiar thickets
of poison oak.

One night, as she toddled
unminded through the house,
I clasped her
by the bold shoulders,

hunting for some Russia
in her bones' shape
and the color of her eyes. "Long Island,"
I pronounced to her gaping stare,

"You're on Long Island,"
while she contemplated me
as curiously as if a bug
crawled across my nose.

When I'm sixty
and she's a perky
Skidmore grad, may our gazes
still cross this lawn

bright with butterflies,
for what the heart brings
to a landscape frees
the landscape, like a river

flowing beyond
the museum's gilt frame
through homelands
quick with history.

Prognosis

Last week he asked straight out
how long he'd live and the doctor
replied that with cancer like his
maybe two years. So now he knows.

He took the news cheerfully
and my sister proclaimed it
a blessing for a man of eighty
with tumors gnawing his spine.

Maybe it's me who can't stand
knowing, pacing off that span:
his first meal taken in the rocker;
first daily walk declined; the *Times*

in bed one morning, then a second,
until his present limping vigor
will seem as distant a year from now
as memories of his eyesight seem today.

To him, two years just means
not now, not on this particular
stretch of rug, with this heave
and clanging drop of the walker.

Specter

You buried your fists
in pillows beside my head
as hair slid into my eyes,

and worked that familiar
slow grind, breasts
tracing my reaching lips,

then dropped your head,
unlocking arms to sprawl,
seconds from sleep.

From your eyes, then,
your movements, and once
or twice even your words,

I knew you belonged to me,
but wake now, dreading
our distance. How furiously

you once loved me, when I
couldn't stall enough,
and now you stall. Tonight

I will touch again the silk
slope of your breast, feel
through fallen hair

the hard bone of your brow,
but in truth I'll flail at empty air,
waking only to these words.

To My Son

I believe there is a disease,
or maybe it was a movie I saw,
where a father who has lost a child
imagines one. You are not
imaginary, but for some time now
I have had to make you up.
You were six when I moved away,
and ever since, for all your
week-end visits and summer stays,
you've become more real to me
in my thoughts
than when you are standing
beside your duffel at my front door.
Walking to class today,
you'd have been amazed
at how much of my concern
swirled around your every step,
though I know that the son I fret over
in my large house and quiet life
is no closer to that young man
crossing the campus quad
than an actor is to his role. Take
my sleepless nights. I replay
my wishes for the life
we could have had,
your needs I could have met,
writhe against
the twist in my heart
that could be straightened

if you would only call. Be glad
you're not here to be a real child
subject to my pain
instead of this shadow
composed of love
and need and pure regret,
too much for human shoulders to bear.

Lullabies

Our stand-bys were folk songs
and early James Taylor, especially
"Sweet Baby James," in which
I'd change "cowboy" to "cowbaby,"
the range to his crib,
and the cattle to his stuffed bear.
I'd part his hair as I sang,
and while he was rarely
asleep when I finished,
he was at least motionless
and watching the ceiling,
fingering his bear's glass eye.

Since then, I've spent so many years
far from him and missed
so many bedtimes
that steering myself back
to those rituals comforts me.
Sometimes when we're together
a song comes on the car radio
and he recognizes it,
the words I changed,
and when there's too little there
for him to retrieve, I prompt him,
restoring the memories we need.

Shitty

In forty years I never heard her utter
a curse stronger than hell or damn
and then only when quoting my father.
Not even a "Christ" after spilling coffee

or "fuck you" to his plaguing criticisms,
until one night after closing her book twice
to rise wincing from the rocker
and answer the phone from his nurse,

the door for his physical therapist,
she stirred again at his shout for food
and limping toward the kitchen said,
"Michael, promise me you won't ever

get old, because you know what it is?"
And I replied no, alert to the rattle
of his walker signaling the daily trek
from bed to living room.

"It's shitty," she said. "Excuse my
profanity, which I don't use often."
I laughed at this modern spark from
a proper elderly soul, grateful

to language for supplying a word
unneeded for eighty-four years,
but now summoned, available, apt.
Then she went to him, shadowing

his treacherous shift from walker
to my arms to automatic chair,
clutching an egg cup filled with
his evening pill cocktail: shitty.

Reveal

When the child went missing
they shouted through rooms
and yard to where the pool
lay uncovered for summer,
flecked with leaves beneath
a massive canopy of trees.
They were fleeing a fear that
others seek their entire lives,
whether in race cars, at war,
or atop Himalayan summits,
when life switches to tragedy
and back like the ball's indecision
in a roulette wheel, or wind
urges a shadow on the water
to identify itself as branch or body.

Ali After Class

Ali, of Indian parents,
hair a black gloss,
the music of Delhi
streaking perfect English,

slinks toward me past
a loud tide of classmates
flooding the hall. She's
in trouble and knows it,

forged a homework excuse,
then bragged too loudly
near adult ears. Last year's
teacher darling

owns a veritable
rap sheet this term:
a boyfriend with a car,
a new giggly impertinence

in class. "I can't get the little
ditherer to shut up,"
gripes Mrs. History,
while Mr. Science

chomps at the chance
to sound jaded: "These kids
stopped being
individuals to me

five years ago. Now
it's a generic child,
you teach the potential,
then they're gone."

To them, Ali's like some
vagrant or hooker
booked on vice sweeps
each election year:

scare 'em/let 'em go. But now
she cringes before me
like a dog about to pee. (Or is this
what the Dean calls

"her cunning,
manipulative way?")
Scolded, she skitters away.
On the kids' side again:

where else to stand?
History with her
honed eyes; Science
booming smoke clouds

of bored sighs: Alis lurk
in their sights, minds,
and dreams; armed each day,
they wake for war.

Without Which

Once you'd have clipped this column
to prop by our front table—"How
Marriages Survive." Now it curls
in my recycling bin like tactics
from a war fresh in memory. Still,
I studied it and bet you did too,
for pointers we already knew—
forbidden topics, the blessings
of compromise—braced by that rock
all collapsed couples admit
has rolled away from their edifice: Love?
No, not love. According to this writer,
will alone makes a marriage fly.
But isn't sticking to it with fierceness
and no love like the circus strongman
wrestling a greased anchor? Surely you and I
still call some feelings by love's name,
though enough had fled to make us
better off apart. But enough of what?
Oh, love's the heart of it. Our new days,
new lives, that withered world
kicked under the carpet—improvements all.
Yet sometimes glancing across
a summer field, I'll think of how
your once great love died, and cry
as for no other loss from that broken time.

For the Best

It's not the decision I doubt—
a custody fight would have
shattered us—but whenever
his mother phones to report
his latest crisis or success
I go weak with regret
that the one son I'll ever have
in the one life I'll ever have
is a shadow, a frustration
of rare visits and rushed calls.

That's when I picture myself
years ago in the courtroom.
I have no questions for that
young father, no accusations
to hurl, just a fascination
at seeing him and imagining
that I might change his mind,
his words. Might, not would—
I always end up accepting that.
I only visit him to make sure
he can still look me in the eye.

Vigil

1. Matter of Time

So this is dying, this cool room
entered during a heat wave
with an air-conditioner blowing
and shades drawn on this man in boxers

with speckled skin and a patch
seeping painkiller into his arm,
who hasn't risen for three days
except to swing his legs over

and trudge, gripping a walker,
into the bathroom. His years,
his lawyer years and golfing years
and drinking years and reading years,

the whole neatly arranged album
was living and this is dying.
As he falls back into bed
I take my leave to find my son

to take his leave; he's with his cousins
in the broiling, bright rest of the house.
Entering, he's thirteen. He'll remember death
as a room with blowing air and towels

protecting the sheets, the need to lie
flat and keep the door closed against
the heat wave in the next room
leveling the rest of the family.

2. Backstory

It grieved me that Dad's nurses knew nothing
of his careers as lawyer/horseman/reader,
just this final role as fertile field for cancer.
Watching them tug his diaper up or bundle sheets
over a soil I wondered if they'd ever pictured
their whimpering culprit in flushed good health
forty years ago, dropping briefcase and *Times*
in the hall before loosening into his rocker
with a book and glass of sherry. Or was their interest
only in this emaciated one abruptly weeping
when rolled onto the latest limb to succumb to tumors?

One night I woke to footsteps in the living room
and imagined Frank, his devoted nurse, studying
photos and inscribed books, retracing eighty years
of pages to illuminate this final chapter. But it was
just Dad, sleepwalking off another painkiller.
Then Frank arrived to clutch his shoulders gently
like a waltzer, explaining the who, why and where
of that confused moment, and lead him back to bed.

3. Object of Affection

The mixture of painkillers and brain lesions
uncorked a vat of anger in him, and he reviled
everyone in scatological terms, especially Frank,
matronly with a pompadour, who lugged him
hourly between bed and toilet, a trek
entailing great pain in limbs choked by cancer.
Since his hiring, Frank had labored wrist-deep
in bodily fluids and insults of the kind that
had scarred my siblings and me for years,
but his resilience surpassed even our
hard-won immunity. *Fairy, fucking fruit*
were names Dad spat while this patient man
lifted him from the wheelchair. After
the drop to the pot, Frank would straighten
and chuckle, "Your father has a way with words."

4. Sole Support

All's fine when Frank swivels
Dad's legs over the bed's edge
and guides him through a stand
and settle into the wheelchair,

and even after the chair bangs
through the bathroom doorway—
Watch your elbows!—all's fine.
Then Frank lowers his neck

to hoist the flimsy body
and the legs come into view, like
sticks with skin, baseball bat slim,
too lean to prop the swaying trunk.

I tug the diaper down fast as
he hangs from Frank's neck
like a baby chimp, then drops hard
to the toilet. Frank withdraws

behind me with the chair,
concerned, questioning, finally
clicking the door shut for privacy.
And we wait in the outer room,

chatting politely to mask the noise,
while listening for a shout, thump,
or more than ten seconds of silence
to bring us barging back in.

5. Coma

By morning Frank couldn't rouse him
and the aide's vigorous primping
failed to make him stir. Then a nurse
arrived and pronounced death imminent,

and said to let him sleep until he died.
When I left he lay as if dozing;
only his breath seemed wakeful,
gulping on the inhale.

The nurse had told us to speak
as if he understood, so I said,
"It's Michael and I'm going," then
"Goodbye, Dad," and "I love you,"

and kissed his gaunt arm, thinking
how thrilled he'd be after all those
thwarted diets. Later, I feared
I'd spoken too softly, though he seemed

to start at my name: maybe a panicked
reach for air, maybe acknowledgment,
or just one last ambiguous signal
that no amount of pondering will ever confirm.

6. Epitaph

You inspired uncommon devotion.
Even at the end, adoring nurses
made your bedsore gleam, clean
as cotton. At your funeral—
three hymns, three passages
of Scripture, and a eulogy
by a minister you'd never met
(you who had scorned religion
the way you scorned ignorance).
I tried to think of one true statement
that would start the heads nodding
of all my siblings, all your friends.
You inspired uncommon devotion. Amen.

III

Two-Score

A quarter-sized sparse spot
where my forelock used to start.
Once shiny bangs now thinned
to strands on my brow. Crescents
like a bowl's imprint circling
my mouth. The skin across
my neck gone crinkly, leather red.
My buttocks hung on their haunches,
as it were, like haunches.
Crossing a ball field, if I leapt
into a sprint my lower back
would sting as after a nine hour drive.

I'd still love to shear half the anxious
thoughts from my head, but know
that no new term, town, or job
will mean a new me. I believe that love
is precious, fragile, hard-earned,
and can almost treat it so. Standing
in life's middle way, I contemplate
forty years of opportunity, both
wasted and awaiting, and find that youth's
a lot like me when I was young: certain
it's unloved, edging apart, until,
unnoticed, it flees without goodbye.

Hamden Imaging

We choose seats beside a couple
in identical denim and ball caps,
the husband blank-faced, present
for moral support, like me. A Hispanic family

of indeterminate make-up
scolds and swaps seats
until a boy's name is called
and they jostle inside.

At the counter, two college students
in neck braces politely describe
"the accident," then sit and gush
over a copy of *Guns and Ammo*:

"Piece of shit" this, "Fuckin' A" that.
A woman peeks in from the hall
and begins to withdraw
when denim wife leaps into

a guffawing reunion—news,
addresses exchanged. "I can't
believe it, it's been fifteen years."
Denim husband stands, smiles,

nods through the introduction,
then sits again heavily,
resuming his boredom.
He's a cop, I now know.

CAT scan, EKG, MRI, X-ray—
a menu of tests hangs
behind the counter. No one's here
for anything minor, except Luis,

who leaves with his entourage,
cleared of mono. And no one's
here alone—even the redneck
stiffnecks keep each other

obnoxious, cursing company.
Mammogram's our curse today,
and when Jeanne emerges grinning
I dismiss this as another

numbing health procedure,
two hour chunk from a day off.
We wait until the parking lot
to cheer her good news,

and only later do I remember
a woman summoned inside
as we arrived, who afterwards
stalked from the office, trailing

no husband or paperwork. Her image
shadows that morning like a cloud
over the sun, spot on a film,
something out of the ordinary.

At the Vietnam Memorial

They hug knees on the cold hill, staring,
five boys, their friends warm on the bus.
They are not all smart but a smart one
is among them, two friendly ones
and a thug in torn leather, and one
so pressured by parents he becomes smart,
a thug, or a best friend on demand. The wind
swims over like a shark to circle,
rustling their collars, and with it, autumn's
hard, heavy dark. Earlier,
they dug fingernails in the letters,
watched others tracing names
with lists and fingers, watched the wheelchairs,
the bandanaed protesters, and three blanketed figures
asleep in the tree-line. My hill provides
a different vantage. I stand by the bus
in sight of them, checking my class list
as the weary seventh grade
quiets behind me. When the stragglers
rise and come, two walking, the others
chasing a ball, shadows have taken
their faces away, and the years
will make them all one—the boys on the bus,
still too young to be sobered by anything,
the boys descending the hill. I won't remember
who ran to the wall, glanced
with polite interest and ran back,
and who approached slowly
the way a crow lands and lingers. One by one
I count them onto the bus, list in hand,
until only the names in their neat,
anonymous rows stare back at me, like the eyes
of an enemy who has just
made his presence known.

By Jenna

Jenna debuted new hair today,
a shorn, black, dramatic bob.
I couldn't recall the old color,

or if her nose ring's hung
since Monday or last year.
We'd only met by sight

until this term, Poetry Elective,
Jenna listening hard, as if
this class, finally, matters.

At hour's end, after my call
for poems, Jenna proffered
two dappled notebooks

and said "You pick." BECAUSE
MEN ARE SHITS, THAT'S WHY,
one entry ends, prefaced by

"To Jeff, George, Rob, Ted, and Colin."
The verb "to hold" recurs ("Hold me";
"I want to be held"), along with

vicious, unrewarding sex,
too much holding
for one sixteen-year-old.

Here, adolescence seems
like some sewer of misery
and low esteem, or is it just

Jenna: heavy, plain,
sharply spoken in an
"I know what you're going

to say" way? YOU NEVER
SPOKE TO OR HEARD ME AT ALL.
I WANT TO DIE THANKS TO YOU.

The second notebook
ends on this, pointing
to a third, or perhaps

just ends, and I shift it,
a sad, slumped thing, into my
"work for tomorrow" pile.

Photograph: First Date

His arms stiffen at his sides
and his fists ball; his chin
pushes down as if a gun
jabbed the back of his head.
His expression pleads
just get it over with
as beside him smiles
the image of feminine poise.

The fumbled corsage,
the hour before her arrival
when he sagged inside his suit
like a doomed man—
he wishes these indignities
would vanish from the memories
of all who witnessed them: him,
his stepmother, her, her mother,
me clicking in the foyer.
But someday he'll beg every second
of this picture back from me,
evidence of his only life.

In the Frame

When the talk swung to horror movies,
a new one where the villain eats the organs
of his victims accompanied by fine wines,

a woman announced that she couldn't
endure such scenes since being raped
some years ago, struck unconscious,

"and when I woke up, they were
heaving me into a truck." Her look back
at our sober looks claimed, "It's nothing

but honesty, and you won't find me
stifling honesty to dine among you."
She recounted her recovery: doctors

and friends, the long climb back
to where she could state
"this happened," and admit

that such words preserved
the recovery. Reeling and spooling,
a man explained—she reeled her life in

from those thugs by spooling it out to us—
until another, reminded of movies again,
changed the subject.

Stepfather

In my dream they're playing catch
while dinner is being made,
as if a place for a father had existed
and this man wandered into it,
saw no one else to fill the role
and picked up the mitt. I know
he's not trying to replace me.
I even like him, chat amiably
when we meet, and couldn't ask
for a better stand-in.
But why should he inherit
what I've spent years
lacking in agony? It's as if
he'd spotted a car I desired
and bought it on impulse,
with found money, though
I've loved it better through craving
than he ever will through driving.

Anorexia

When Christie rolled up
by me at the Willow stop,
our looks-both-ways met,
springing happy waves:
my sweetest student
in a class she loves.
I swung the car, low
with groceries, into the turn,
and checked behind
for churning rollerblades,
saw legs still sticklike, arms
white pipes, black helmet
swallowing a skull. No
bones showed, though;
enough fat carpeted them
to cloak blue veins
that shocked the eye
last spring. All summer,
Christie's fourteenth, went to save
that lace-frail body.

This fall she just seems
skinny, face grayed
as if by stone, but
no less meek or happy.
I study what I studied
in the car mirror, her body
like a thing apart, as a doctor
views a body, a mortician,
Saint Laurent. Then Christie
battles through, all
smiles and grace, as in her
teasing surge to catch me

on the rollerblades, coasting
finally, with a laugh
and wave, unmistakably,
in the mirror, her.

Burial

After the last word of the last prayer,
when the familiars stretched their necks
and to avoid looking at him
looked at their cars, he pointed his eyes
at a grove of oak flaming with sunlight
where a shirtless youth
wove a lawnmower around trees,
strewing wigs of cut grass. The air and sun
hugged him away from sound
until he saw his new world as new,
marveling at how a man can shrink down
around one fact of disbelief: *my son is dead.*

Soon a reception would start in the house of friends;
he must rise from this borrowed stone,
force will through nerves to muscles,
move a step, endure the day, release
to darkness the disheveled grave.
It was not possible. It was just not possible.

At Anchor

On a ledge formed by the skin
of her hip veering in to meet
her ribcage, a handle of flesh
which, if she were younger,
vainer, more gym-obsessed,
or hadn't borne three children,
might not exist, gives the grip
I want, as unmistakably her
as her handwriting or first name.
Just flexing my fingers lets me
conjure that place out of sense
and thought until I'm as good
as clutching it when she's away. And love.
Love, too, is necessary for this
act of prestidigitation to occur.

To My Son's Girlfriend

I'm tempted to ask
what you see in him.
Although you probably
see the good that I see
I wonder if you realize
how much he is my handiwork,
or which of the qualities
you daydream about in class
are ones that I take pride in,
his cordiality, for example,
or love of silliness.

It's uncomfortable for me
to think of anyone else
loving him the way I do,
possessing him in a way
that only his mother and I
have ever possessed him,
and I can't deny being jealous,
not so much reluctant
to share or relinquish him
as resolved to remind you
that he's been around
longer than your love,
under construction if you will,
and that each cute trait
or whatever occurs to you
when you hear his name
I feel proprietary about,
like a woodworker
who makes a table
intending to sell it
but prays that no buyer
will recognize its worth.

At the Mall

As we plod through the gleaming atrium,
forlornness in love makes his feet drag
and his words slow and sputter. In cargo pants,
fleece vest and bleached hair, he's a man at thirteen—
another inch and he'll look me in the eye.
Passing schoolmates with subtle friendly
or disdainful glances, he's half-impatient
with my teasing and unkemptness and, worse,
today I'm offering a sermon on morality,
the difference between shock and art,
begun at home when he played a rap CD
with lyrics so foul-mouthed I refused
to listen. "O.k., o.k., Dad," he muttered,
switching it off, and now turns to me
with a look of self-assurance and asks
"Did your parents like your music?"
sulking as we elbow through the Food Court.
I've learned to stand patiently on the shore
of these silences: yesterday in the car
he erupted from one to blurt his anxiety
over the Valentine's Day dance: he doesn't like
the girl who asked him and dares not ask
the girl he likes. My consolation sounded
useless to us both. Was it ever easier?
I remember him at three months, squalling on a sofa
during an August heat wave. After midnight
I scooped him up, propped us both
in front of an Ingrid Bergman movie
until his relentless wails and my fatigue
made me hurry him to the town reservoir
where we strolled the walkway for an hour,
him bumping to sleep on my shoulder.
I never thought to rejoice then that the cure
for what ailed him lay within my powers,

in the blessings of motion and silence
that fail to soothe us as we circle this mall,
where both his body and his anguish
have grown too heavy for my arms.

In Class

Boys will label
another boy gay
if he likes a poem

or sneer
when a girl says
something soulful,

but this is trickier,
these girls snickering
brow to brow over

a comment by a girl
who just last week
was their best friend.

Girls mocking boys
I can scold my way
out of; boys calling

each other stupid
is nothing a good
recess won't cure,

but this girl on girl—
what would I call it?—
this is nuclear.

This Way

You have this way when I try
to provoke or reproach you
without letting you catch me at it
of re-shaping my words
so they point me out
to myself as an idiot,
leaving you, or my image of you,
off to one side giving
a raised-brow questioning look
that asks is this what you want?

Which is the question
I was asking of myself
even while fanning
my childish controversy,
and of you, as in will you
take me like this, and you do.

On the Phone

That whooshing, watery,
radio-being-tuned sound
tells me he's outdoors
on his way somewhere
and I'd better talk fast.
I can't remember
the last time I phoned him
without dreading that countdown
to when he says, "I'm going
into the subway, Dad, got to go."
Lately, he even calls me from the street—
a convenient way to keep
his keeping in touch short. He's right—
I'd talk to him for an hour,
marching through my pent-up questions.
It tires me, wanting him so much,
the resistance with which he responds.
I bet there's a girl out there
he'd duck into a lobby
to keep speaking to
as long as she desired. Instead,
he tells me that I'm breaking up,
and there's a sound
as if he's dropped the phone
into a rushing river, which then
pulls him in too, his life.

Teller

You were neither made
nor made up to be here,

spinning in your chair
to type in my account number

while nursing a mood
that I'd describe

as halfway between
indifference and a sulk.

You look as if you want
to be looked at,

with your tan, arms
laden with bangles,

and leather mini-skirt,
but act as if not.

You're too many things for me
to expect you'll notice me—

too young, too bored,
too coiffed, manicured

and blushed. You've primped for the prom
and this is the credit union.

Are you bound for a better life
or lacking in acceptance?

Or just waiting,
if not for me,

then for a handsome guy your own age,
or happiness,

in which case I admire you
for making yourself presentable

in this least likely place
for it to appear,

though when you rip my slip
from the dot-matrix printer,

slap it on the counter
and ask me to step

to one side, I'm happy
to oblige.

Accompaniment

You sit between two women in a restaurant,
bare arms on the table, and if I sat beside you
I'd run my fingers up them into your sleeve.
You think of me as you talk, just as I began
to write this while writing something else. All day
I've tried to decide whether I love you and whether
to say so: I must because the thought of that sleeve
makes my heart clench and I want to shatter this desk
with my hand. As dinner ends you imagine what
we might do at this hour in this town, but I'm
stuck on that sleeve, the turn of your shoulder
underneath it where the cloth halts my hand
like a leash, sending it back down over your arm's
pink gardening tan, along the hair of your wrist—like gold
now glinting, now invisible in a sand river. As you pause
outside the restaurant, battling an umbrella, I try
to untrack myself, to say what needs saying, decide
like fingers lost along a surface overwhelming
to their touch, or like a woman testing for rain,
whether I'm in or out, staying or going.

Blessed

Mornings she clambers
onto me at nine, face
in full smile, and lays
her long length against

my longer one, arms
stretched, hands clasped,
toes to toes. I rest
my cup on her back

and our talk's never
easier than then,
picking from the ash
of late night thoughts

warm chips, fanning
the tiniest sparks
of our planned days.
We lay last night

trawling rice cakes
through butter,
chipped enough crumbs
to keep her picking

at my chest and the dogs
on full scrap alert. Traffic
rushed like water,
dwindled and died. She slept

and I slept and woke
twined in her limbs. Into his world
God has built
such grounds for joy.

Inspiration

It used to be as easy as filling
the family pool in spring.
I'd absent myself for a while,
then return when the level had risen.

I don't know if I'm depleted, dry,
or onto something more subtle
than effusiveness these days,
but this pool's no longer filling.

I wouldn't say it's empty. More like
a mine with a rescuer at the top
listening through a stethoscope
for the quietest sound worth hearing.

Just a Minute

After all my failed loves
I hoped that this might be the one
I could retire on, the one that worked,
making the others worth the pain.
I was only counting on a moment,
just one time when I'd pause and take stock,
thinking how happy I felt
with life a warm gust at my back.
I even had a setting—
a café in Greece one hot morning
as we finish breakfast
and sit planning the day. We're older
and no longer covet anything
except this trip and each other
and we don't care how we look,
but the sex is still good. The age we are
is still years away, and that feeling
has always seemed no less distant,
something to work toward slowly
as a kind of last chance for happiness
so don't rush it. But then yesterday
on your quick visit from out of town
we found an afternoon and evening
to do nothing together—nap and cook
and find something unsatisfactory on TV,
and lying beside you on the rug
I made my usual visit to that golden years moment,
wondering if I'd recognize it
when it happened—I always fear
that at the end of life I'll regret
not having savored such times,
the way I feel I never acknowledged
and basked in my twenties.
Just then I realized that maybe this half-day

in our long distance relationship
was that moment, arrived prematurely
and gaping for attention like a baby.
I shook myself and sat up
and looked around and kissed you
and memorized the place and time.
I had you and wanted nothing.
The future was the fantasy,
a hope for a memory
of when one had received life's grace
open-armed, open-eyed, and open-hearted.

Location, Location

A spider webbed the cellar doorway
the morning of my cleaning spree,
pale star with him floating at the center.
And for all his meanness, bigness,
blackness, I let him be, having once
squashed ants, crushed butterflies,
stalking field and sidewalk. Love,
come late in life, had softened all
my anger. His net spanned half
the upper frame, invisible as water,
and forgetting to bend I swept it
down with my hair. When I looked up,
he clung to wood by an arm like one
leapt to safety above the falls. Next day
he watched from his new web like an eye
as I remembered and ducked, but again
my head brushed his rigging down.
I wanted to flick or kick him, saying
(I did say) "You just can't live here now,"
or stomp and be done, but left him
gripping the lintel like a kitten.
On the third day he'd climbed onto
the propped screen door and strung
his web across its pane, tied prettily
to all four corners: safer, better off.
The way I see him now contents me,
swinging in his hammock as I gently
close the screen. Our bond's in where
we've come from, which makes
our current condition so sweet.

Michael Milburn teaches high school English in New Haven, Connecticut. He previously taught writing at Syracuse University and at Yale. His first book of poems, *Such Silence*, won the Alabama Poetry Award and was published by the University of Alabama Press in 1989. His book of essays, *Odd Man In*, won the First Series Award in Creative Nonfiction and was published by Mid-List Press in 2004.

Breinigsville, PA USA
27 August 2009
223088BV00001B/14/P